Whales

Consultant editor
Henry Pluckrose

Illustrated by
Norman Weaver

Gloucester Press · New York · 1979
Copyright © The Archon Press Ltd 1979

Blue whale

Fin whale

Right whale

Humpback

Sei whale

Bryde's whale

Whales

"DISCARD"

Published in the United States by
Gloucester Press, in 1979
All rights reserved

Originated by David Cook and
Associates and produced by
The Archon Press Ltd
70, Old Compton Street
London W1V 5PA

First published in
Great Britain 1979 by
Hamish Hamilton Children's Books Ltd
Garden House, 57-59 Long Acre
London WC2E 9JL

Printed in Great Britain by
W S Cowell Ltd
Butter Market, Ipswich

Certain illustrations originally published in
The Closer Look Series

Library of Congress
Catalog Card Number: 78-73840
ISBN: 0-531-03428-3
ISBN (Lib. Bdg.): 0-531-03406-2

The Blue whale lives in the cold, southern waters of the Antarctic.
It is the biggest living animal on earth.
It can weigh as much as ten elephants put together.

These whales are all drawn
to the same scale.
The Blue whale is the biggest.

This Humpback whale is jumping into the air.
When he returns to the water
he makes a very big splash indeed.
Sometimes whales leap to impress their mates
and sometimes just for fun.
Big whales spend the summers in the cold
polar seas of the Arctic and Antarctic.
In the polar winters they travel to the
warm tropical oceans where they breed.

Whales are not fish, even though they live in water.
Whales are mammals, warm-blooded creatures who bear their young alive and feed them on milk.
This Bottlenose dolphin is a kind of whale.

Fish are scaly but whales are covered with soft skin.
Fish breathe through gills, but whales have lungs and breathe in and out through a blow hole on top of their heads.

One family of whales, the Mysticetes, have no teeth.
Instead a mesh of whalebone hangs down inside their mouths.
This acts as a net in which they trap the shrimps and other small sea creatures (called plankton) on which they feed.

Right whale

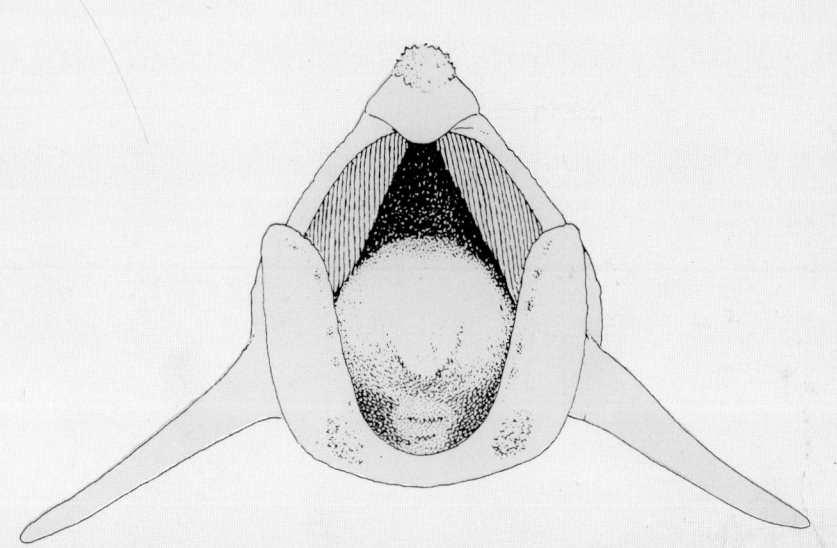

Front view of the open mouth of a Right whale.

Rorqual whale

The Right whale was the whale most often caught by the early hunters.
It was slow moving and easy to harpoon.
It floated when captured so it was easy to tow ashore.

Its whalebone was used to make many of the things we now make out of plastic. Its oil was used for lighting and heating. These whales have been hunted so much that they are now very rare.

Rorquals are fast moving and can travel at nearly 20 miles per hour.
However, they spend much of their time rolling lazily through the surface waters, gulping down enormous mouthfuls of plankton as they go.

Rorquals live in groups called pods.
There are different kinds of Rorquals
such as the Blue whales and the Finbacks.
These are Finback whales.
They are only a bit smaller than
the Blue whales.

The baby whale is called a calf.
The calf is born tail first because if
his head emerged first, he might drown
before he reached the surface.
As he cannot suck, his mother
squirts her milk into his mouth.

Most whales move about in family groups.
The whales in the picture are Humpbacks.
They are moving to the cold Arctic
waters where they will spend the summer.
Their thick fat, called blubber,
keeps whales warm.

Sperm whales do not feed on plankton.
They eat squid which they catch far below
the surface of the sea.
Because it is so dark there, they use
sound waves (like radar) to detect
their prey.
Sperm whales can stay underwater for an
hour without surfacing for air.

Giant squid

The dolphin is also a member of the whale family.
Most dolphins live in the warmer oceans of the world and feed on fish which they catch near the surface.
They travel in big groups called schools.
There can be thousands of dolphins in a school.

23

There are many different kinds of dolphins.
Here are just a few of them.

Common dolphin   Bottlenose dolphin

White-sided dolphin   Commerson's dolphin   Hourglass dolphin

Dolphins are often friendly to people.
The picture below shows a dolphin
called Opo who lived in the sea near
a town in New Zealand.
She liked children and sometimes
she even gave them short rides
on her back.

Small whales and dolphins can be kept in captivity.
They can be trained to do tricks and seem to enjoy their work.
The Pilot whale here is jumping for a fish.
The dolphins are just having fun.

Pilot whale

Pacific dolphins

Killer whales are the biggest of all the dolphins.
They hunt in packs, usually of less than a dozen but sometimes numbering 30 or 40. They are very common in the Arctic and the Antarctic.

Killer whales eat seals, penguins, fish and even other whales.
When they see penguins on the ice they come up from underneath them, smashing the ice with their heads and tossing the penguins into the water.

Whales are valuable to man.
We can get a wide range of materials
from them to use in such things as soap,
paint, cosmetics, drugs, dyes, fertilizers,
animal foods and glue.
But if we kill too many whales
they may disappear altogether like the
dinosaurs.

Index

Antarctic, 7, 8, 19, 26
Arctic, 8, 19, 26

blubber, 19
Blue whale, 6, 7, 17
Bottlenose dolphin, 10, 23

calves, 18
Commerson's dolphin, 23
Common dolphin, 23

dolphins, 22-3, 24-5

Finback whales, 17
fish, 10, 11, 27

Hourglass dolphin, 23
Humpback whale, 8
hunting, 14, 15

Killer whales, 26-7

mammals, 10
Mysticetes, 12

New Zealand, 24

Opo, 24

Pacific dolphins, 25
Pilot whale, 25
plankton, 12, 16, 19
pods, 17
products, from whales, 15, 28

Right whales, 12, 14-15
Rorqual whales, 13, 16-17

schools, 22
seals, 27
Sperm whales, 20
squid, 20, 21

White-sided dolphin, 23

599
PLU
PLUCKROSE, Henry

WHALES

"DISCARD"

ST. JAMES SCHOOL
LIBRARY
ST. CATHARINES, ONT.